Prita Goes to India

To Prita, Amrita and my wife for their forbearance,
and to Janetta, Yvonne and Judith for their invaluable support.

First published in Great Britain in 2005 by Frances Lincoln Children's Books,
4 Torriano Mews, Torriano Avenue, London NW5 2RZ

www.franceslincoln.com

Distributed in the USA by Publishers Group West

British Library Cataloguing in Publication Data available on request

ISBN 1-84507-128-X

Printed in Singapore
1 3 5 7 9 8 6 4 2

Prita Goes
to India

Prodeepta Das

FRANCES LINCOLN CHILDREN'S BOOKS

Delhi

Agra

INDIA

Orissa

Cuttack

Puri

I'm so excited. Mama and Papa are taking my sister Apa and me to India! They want to show us some of the great sights and the places in Orissa where they grew up. It will be the most exciting journey I've ever done, so I've decided to write everything down in my new holiday diary…

Delhi

It was morning when our plane touched down in Delhi.
As I stepped out, the hot, stuffy air smacked my cheeks.
Porters rushed towards us with trolleys.

And there was Papa's friend
Uncle Devdas waiting for us
with Auntie Veena.

His house was an
hour's drive away.

He gave us a big welcome – in India, guests are very
important people – and offered us the main bedroom.
We have our own air-conditioning.

Agra

Today we went to Agra to see the Taj Mahal.
Apa says that it's one of the wonders of the world.

To stop pollution, no motor vehicles are allowed within two miles of the Taj. When we reached Agra, we took an auto-rickshaw. The road was so bumpy, I felt as if I was going to fall out of the side!

On the way, we saw working elephants walking along the side of the road.

Once we were inside the monument, we had to take off our shoes and wear special cloths over our feet. It was hot, but through the lattice-work cooler air filtered in from the Yamuna river behind the Taj.

The train to Orissa

Mama's village in the state of Orissa is a long way from Delhi, and we're stopping off at Cuttack on the way. Even on the Rajdhani Express, the journey takes 24 hours. The station was crowded with people asleep on their luggage, waiting for trains.

Apa bagged the upper bunk in our sleeping compartment, and we played games and drew pictures. Later on, we ate the *chappatis* (flat breads) and curries that Auntie Veena had packed for us. Poor Papa had a tummy upset and had to survive on biscuits and a banana.

This morning, I was woken by a voice calling "*Chai!*", "*Kafi!*" ("tea!", "coffee!"). A man was carrying small cups in a bucket and two large kettles. All day vendors went up and down the train selling magazines, nuts and snacks.

I sat by the window watching paddy fields, cattle and villages go by. I'd been told that there was a big river called the Mahanadi before we reached Cuttack. So every time we went over a long bridge, I asked Mama, "Is this the big river?"

Cuttack

Mama and Papa have lots of relations at Cuttack and they've all asked us to stay. Our first stop was with Papa's elder cousin, Cuttack Bapa and his wife, Cuttack Bou. While we were with them, their daughter brought her baby son to see us. I played with him and watched him being bathed. He's a very happy baby and didn't cry once!

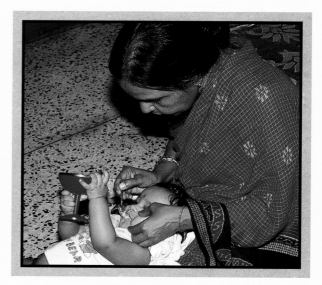

We spent a day with Papa's younger cousin, Chandan Dada, his wife Baby Khudi and their son Puchu. Like many children in India, Puchu studies hard and has extra lessons every day after school. But he was so excited to see us, he decided to miss school just this once. We played Chinese Chequers and Brain Vita, an Indian version of Solitaire.

It was fun squatting on the floor and eating *baras* – a savoury batter of black beans fried in oil – and other nice things that Main, another auntie, cooked for us.

(The recipe for baras is on page 34.)

In the afternoon, Dengu Mamu (Mama's brother) took Apa and me to look around Cuttack.

On our way back, the sky clouded over and the monsoon rain thundered down. It was fierce compared to drizzles in England.

We took shelter in a roadside stall serving chai.

Janla

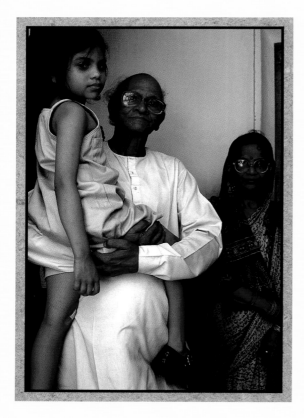

Our next trip was to Janla, Mama's village, to see Ajini and Aai, my grandpa and grandma, and my great-grandmother, Boda Aai. The sound of our car brought Ajini and Aai out on to the verandah. "We've been waiting so long to see you!" he said. He picked me up and gave me a hug.

As soon as we'd unpacked, I took out the box of biscuits we'd brought from London and gave it to Ajini.

The next morning, Ajini and Dengu Mamu took me to see the local rice-fields – lots of small plots of land divided by narrow ridges, where rainwater collects. Dengu Mamu carried me over the wet parts!

Yesterday everyone celebrated the festival of Rakhi. A *rakhi* is a decorated piece of sacred thread which girls tie on their brothers' wrists to bring them good luck. The girls get presents in return. I bought the nicest rakhis I could find for my cousins.

We went on a picnic to Nandan Kanan, an animal park near Bhubaneswar, Orissa's capital city. Ajini's friend, who was the local vet, showed us a young tiger recovering from illness – she lapped up a bowl of milk in no time at all!

That night was a special one in Orissa. It was Khudurkuni Puja, when Hindus worship the goddess Khudurkuni. Girls wearing their new clothes pray for health and happiness. Apa and I went to the goddess's shrine and offered a ripe coconut.

I loved the windowsill in the upstairs bedroom
where we slept! I liked to sit and write postcards
to my child-minder, Auntie Sharon, and to all
my friends in London.

In the mornings I sat
watching the women
filling their big buckets
and pitchers with drinking
water at the tube well.

Widows in India wear simple
white sarees. Boda Aai was
overwhelmed by the new saree
we brought her from Delhi.
"It's lovely!" she said.

Then she hugged me, took me on her
lap and told me how different life was
when she was my age. In those days,
girls didn't go to school; instead, her
mother taught her how to cook and
help around the house.

Puri

When they're in Orissa, Mama and Papa always visit Puri. As well as having a beautiful beach, Puri is one of the four most sacred Hindu places, with a temple to Jagannath, Lord of the Universe.

On our way there, we stopped by a cyclist selling *poida*, green coconuts. "My favourite!" said Papa, and we bought some.

Near the temple was a big bazaar. We bought presents there for Auntie Sharon and my friends. I loved the masks of Jagannath and bought two.

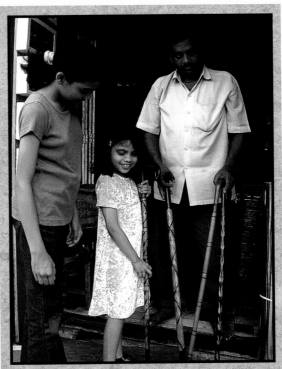

Khudi Aai, Ajini's auntie, asked us to buy her a walking stick, so Apa and I chose one in a cane shop nearby.

This morning, we went for a walk along the beach. The fishing boats were coming in and people were pulling the long nets ashore.

I saw a man making sand sculptures of faces and temples. I've never seen anything like that in England! His name was Sudarsan Pattanaik and he has won lots of awards for his sculptures.

Mama and I walked out towards the waves. Suddenly, a very high wave hit us and dragged us into the sea! Papa came running. Then a *nolia* (life guard) pulled Mama and me to safety. Papa thanked the *nolia* and gave him some money for helping us.

On our way back to Janla,
we stopped at two villages.
At the first one, craftsmen were
making *pattachitras* – cloths
covered with rice-paste pictures
from Hindu religious stories.

The second village
was full of shops
selling colourful
patchwork.

Today it was time to say goodbye. Ajini and Aai packed homemade pickles and sweets for us to take back with us. Our whole family came to be photographed and I took a picture. In India, "family" means not only the father, mother and their children, but all the relations as well!

Then everyone said goodbye to us at Cuttack station. Their love had bound me so close to them, I wanted to stay. As I stood looking out of the train door and waving goodbye, I couldn't hold back my tears.

I hope one day I will come back to India.

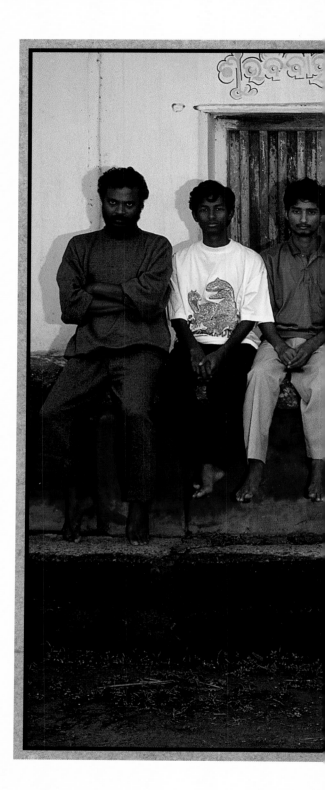

Baras cooked for Prita

Recipe by Kaumudi Das

Serves 4

You'll need:

- ◆ 150g skinless *urad daal* (split white lentils)
- ◆ 500 ml vegetable oil
- ◆ 1/2 tsp salt
- ◆ 2 green chillies
- ◆ 1 small onion
- ◆ 2 sprigs coriander leaves
- ◆ 1 tbsp finely-chopped fresh ginger

+ a grown-up on hand to help you with the frying.

1. Soak urad daal in plenty of water for six hours
    or overnight.

2. Wash urad daal thoroughly in cold water four or five times,
    until the water runs clear.

3. Grind the soaked and washed urad daal in a food processor,
    gradually adding 5 tablespoonfuls of cold water until it forms
    a smooth paste.

4. Empty into a container, add salt and stand for 1 hour.

5. Add chopped ginger, finely-chopped onion and sliced chillies.

6. Make the paste into small balls and flatten them.

7. Ask a grown-up to heat the oil in a saucepan until it is
    almost smoking and then reduce to medium heat.

8. Deep fry the baras until they are golden brown

9. Serve with coconut chutney.

Glossary

Agra - northern Indian city famous for the Taj Mahal, one of the most beautiful buildings in the world. It was built by the Emperor Shah Jahan in memory of his wife, using white marble and gemstones.

auto-rickshaw - three-wheeled, hooded scooter adapted to carry up to four passengers. It is much cheaper and slower than a taxi.

chappati - pancake made from wheat flour, cooked without oil or butter.

Cuttack - ancient capital of Orissa.

Delhi - capital city of India.

Jagannath - Hindu God who is the Lord of the Universe.

Khudurkuni Puja - special day for worshipping Khudurkuni, a form of the powerful Hindu goddess Durga.

Mahanadi river - longest river in Orissa. It is nearly two miles across at its widest.

Main - Auntie.

monsoon - wind that brings the rainy season after the scorching Indian summer.

Orissa - Indian state on the east coast, famous for its beaches, beautiful saris, temples and nature reserves.

paddy fields - fields where rice plants grow.

Puri - town on the east coast of Orissa, famous for its beautiful beach and its temple to Jagannath, an important Hindu god.

Rajdhani Express - fast train which runs from Delhi to Orissa's *rajdhani* (capital city), Bhubaneswar.

Rakhi - thin sacred string which a girl ties around her brother's wrist to bring him good luck.

saree - a long cotton, silk or nylon material which women wear.

tube well - a tube pushed several feet into the ground to bring out safe water for people to drink and use. In many parts of India there is no regular water supply.

vendors - people who sell things by travelling from place to place and house to house.

working elephants - elephants used for carrying people and their luggage, and for moving logs through forests.

Index